AF260743

Freestyle: The Israel Adesanya Story
by David Riley

First edition 2022

ISBN 978-1-99-116224-3

Text © 2022 David Riley
Illustrations © 2022 Ant Sang
Designed and typeset by Bronwen Billinghurst (i-set-type)
Edited by Sue Copsey (www.suecopsey.com)



Thank you: Israel Adesanya, Cara Bareman, Eugene Bareman, Bronwen Billinghurst, Ant Sang, Sue Copsey, Gary Wilson

# Freestyle
## The Israel Adesanya Story

By David Riley

Illustrated by Ant Sang

Boom! Tick!  Boom! Tick!
Boom! Tick!
Boom-tick-tick!

Three men dressed in camo gear emerge through a tunnel into the arena. They're dance friends of Israel Adesanya.

Tonight, Israel fights for the UFC middleweight championship of the world.

Israel joins them.

They huddle-lock arms-bounce-bounce-split! Boom! Tick! Boom-tick!

They begin to dance. There's not one style — it's capoeira, krump, kapa haka. Flex-spin-machine gun-pukana! The dance finishes with each man's arm stretched to the sky, reaching for all the power of heaven, sending it to Israel.

"You're gonna get smashed, Izzy!" yells a fan.

"That's not what I see," Israel thinks to himself.

He hugs his coach and the rest of his team and steps into the Octagon.

Sixty-thousand fans have filled the stadium. Millions around the world are watching.

It's the **biggest moment** of Israel's life.

The announcer shouts into his microphone:

"Iiiiiiiiiiiit's ... tiiiiiiiiime!"

STY

NARUTO
2

Israel was born in Lagos, the largest city in Nigeria, Africa, on 22 July 1989, the oldest of five children. His dad's name is Femi. He's an accountant. His mum's name is Taiwo. She's a nurse.

Israel's family belongs to the Yoruba cultural group of Nigeria. His full name is:

## Israel Mobolaji Temitayo Odunayo Oluwafemi Owolabi Adesanya.

Growing up, Israel loved reading **manga** (comics) and watching **anime** (cartoons).

He played video games like Fight Night on Game Boy.

And he learned Taekwondo, a fighting sport that includes jumping, kicking and spinning.

One time he did a back flip off the couch and broke a vase, a window and his arm.

**"You're not doing any more of this!"** said his mum.

Israel's parents wanted him to do well at school.

They helped him with his homework and bought lots of books for him to read.

But reading was hard for Israel. That's because he has **dyslexia**. People with dyslexia sometimes see letters moving around when they're reading.

That can make them feel frustrated, angry or sad.

**"Is there something wrong with me?"**
Israel asked his teacher.

**"No,"** she said. "You just see things differently.

**Dyslexic people have done great things in our world.**

**You can too."**

When Israel was ten, his family left Nigeria. Femi and Taiwo wanted their children to see more of the world.

First, they moved to Ghana, another African country not far from Nigeria.

At his new school, Israel met some friends who loved to dance. One of them taught him moves called **popping** and **locking**.

Popping and locking taught Israel how to control his body.

His mum was happy about that!

Then they moved to Rotorua, New Zealand.

Israel found it hard to fit in at first. Some children were mean to him, just because he was different.

"They tripped me up when I walked to class, spat at me, and threw things at me from a bus," he says.

One Saturday a boy biked past Israel's house shouting, "Do you ride lions and elephants?" and, "Do you swing on trees?"

**"Why is he doing that?"** Israel wondered.

**"I don't even know him."**

The boy with the bike went to the same school as Israel. One day he yelled, "Why don't you go back to Africa?"

The boy's friends started laughing.

Then he pushed Israel over.

Israel felt confused, sad, and angry. Without thinking, he hit the boy.

Then he started crying.

"My parents didn't teach me to act like this," he thought to himself.

He ran to the library, a place he always felt safe. There, he started reading his favourite Calvin and Hobbes comic book. Wow … Calvin was being bullied too!

How did Calvin respond to the bullying? He dreamed up stories starring himself as:

**a dinosaur who crushes every opponent
a space traveller exploring the universe
a giant spider hunting prey.**

"Dreaming is so cool," Israel thought.

**"In my imagination,
I can go ANYWHERE
and be ANYTHING!"**

When Israel went to high school, he still felt like an outsider.

**"I was like a bat among doves,"** he says.

One day his school held a talent competition, and Israel did a dance to Michael Jackson's song, *"Wanna Be Startin' Somethin"*.

The students whooped when he started popping and locking. But then he did a body wave … and they went crazy!

"Gbe body*!" he said, as he rippled across the floor.

**"Whoooaaaah, I never knew he could do that!"** someone yelled.

"They really like the way I perform," Israel thought as he moonwalked off the stage.

### "And I love to do it!"

*Gbe body is Nigerian slang meaning, move your body, move your feet, move your soul.

"Israel, we want you to go to university," said Mum one day. "You can be a physician, a lawyer, an engineer or even an accountant, like Dad."

"That's why we came to New Zealand," said Dad. "To give you a good future."

"I don't know what I want to be yet," Israel said. **"But I'm going to have a big future."**

Later that week, he watched a film called Ong-Bak: Muay Thai Warrior.

"I want to be a fighter, like that guy!" he thought. So he joined a Muay Thai gym.

Israel also liked watching UFC fights on YouTube.

"It would be awesome to do that," he thought. "But you probably have to be big, muscly and aggressive, like action-movie characters. That's not me."

Israel's favourite fighter was Anderson 'The Spider' Silva. Anderson wasn't big, muscly or aggressive. He was calm. And he won by knockout, 22 times!

"He's a skinny kid, like me," Israel said. **"If he can do it, so can I."**

Israel entered a fighting competition. He thought his kickboxing training and watching YouTube videos would be enough preparation.

It wasn't.

He lost every round.

"I'm not discouraged," he thought to himself.

# "I know I can do this."

One morning, about a month later, Israel knocked on his parents' bedroom door.

"I'm moving to Auckland," he said. "I want to be a fighter."

Mum spilled her cup of water on the floor.

"What! Where will you live?" said Dad.

"In my car, if I have to."

Mum started crying. "What about university?" she said.

"That's not my dream."

"What if it doesn't work out?" said Dad. "Then what?"

"It will work out."

Israel went to a gym in Auckland called City Kickboxing (CKB). It's run by Eugene Bareman, one of the best martial arts trainers in the world.

"What do you want to get out of this?" Eugene said.

"I want to be the UFC middleweight champion of the world."

**"You're crazy!"** Eugene said. "But we can work with that."

Israel found a job in a call centre. He trained at CKB every day after work. First kickboxing. Then learning how to punch correctly. Then Jiu Jitsu.

One time after training, Israel sat next to the water cooler, and stared at the city through the large window.

**"I will be the UFC middleweight champ,"** he said to himself.

By 2013, Israel felt he had to make some changes to achieve his goal of being a UFC champion.

First, he **quit his job** ... and became a full-time fighter.

"Son, what are you doing!" said Mum.

"I had to do it," Israel says. "I wasn't happy in that job, and too many people are doing jobs they're not happy in."

Then he did something that really shocked his parents. He moved to China! He did that to compete against more fighters.

While he was there, Israel fought 24 times in 8 months.

**He won most of his fights.** He respected his opponents, **bowed** to them, **helped them up**, and **hugged** them.

He loved to entertain the fans too. He lay on top of the ropes after a win, and sometimes breakdanced in the ring.

Chinese fans loved Israel and his performing style of fighting.

They named him, **'Black Dragon'.**

Around this time, Israel chose his nickname,

# 'The Last Stylebender'.

He got the idea from one of his favourite TV programmes: *Avatar: The Last Airbender.*

"I related to the character Aang," he says. "Especially his quest to achieve his destiny. He has to master all the elements — fire, water, earth and air. I have to master all the martial arts to achieve my destiny."

Israel came back to New Zealand and trained harder than ever before.

**Cycle.**

**Punching bag.**

**Wheelbarrow.**

**Weights.**

**Ropes.**

One on one with Eugene: **"Dig it in! Boom-boom-boom! Big effort! Don't be scared! Fatigue yourself!"**

Group training with other fighters: **"Pressure them! Take him down! Move-explode-turn!**

# Punch-punch-PUNCH!"

THUMP!

"How come you don't dance in the ring anymore?" asked Israel's trainer one day.

"People are saying I'm too cocky," Israel said.

**"Don't let them change you,"** said the trainer.

## "Be yourself."

Israel had read the same message in a book called *The Mastery of Love*, by Don Ruiz. *Happiness can only come from inside of you and is the result of your love, Don wrote. You are responsible for your happiness.*

Israel was also inspired by a boxer named Prince Naseem Hamed, who was known for his spectacular entrances:

- sitting on a flying carpet
- carried in on a golden palanquin
- acting out a scene from Michael Jackson's *Thriller*.

"Prince Naseem is having a lot of fun being himself," Israel thought.

**"I need to love myself and my expression of fighting."**

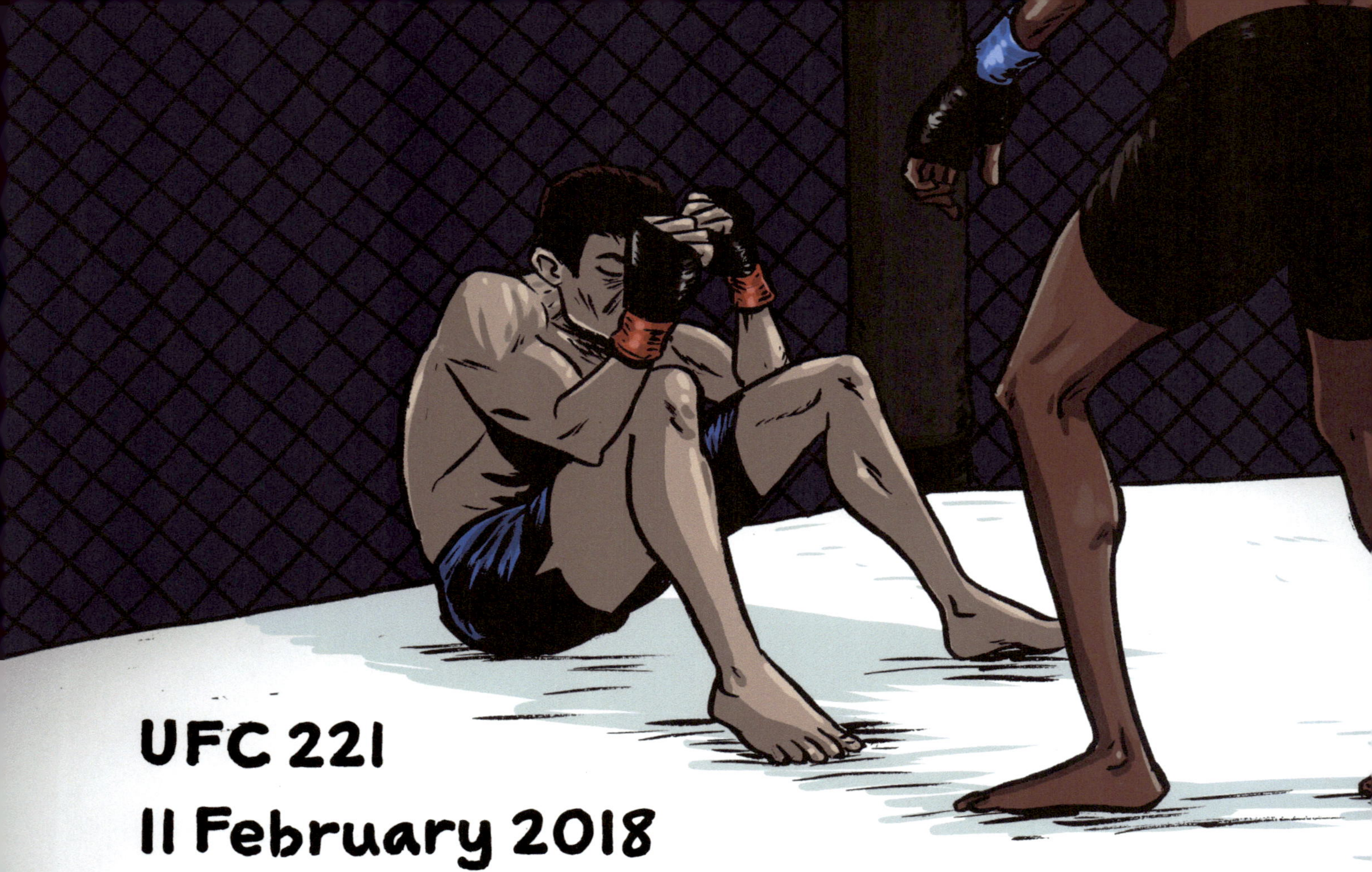

# UFC 221
# 11 February 2018

At last, after years of training and battling, Israel made it to the UFC.

He wanted to do a dramatic walkout for his first fight, to show the world who he was, like Prince Naseem did. Maybe a dance?

"No," said the UFC boss. "Fight fans don't want to see men dancing."

Israel's opponent was Rob 'Razor' Wilkinson. Rob was good at wrestling and Jiu Jitsu. In round one, they grappled, they scuffled, they tangled.

"Enough of that!" Eugene said between rounds. "Show him what you have!"

**PEOWNNNNNN!** sounded the horn to start round two.

Israel's kicks, jabs and knees slammed into Rob's legs, pummelled into his ribs, rumbled off his face. Rob covered his head, folded into a ball and sank down, down, down to the floor.

The referee raised Israel's arm in the air. **Winner by TKO!**

## "I'm the new dog in the yard!"

Israel yelled.

Israel won four UFC fights in 2018. He made it into the UFC video game. And he was named Breakthrough Fighter of the Year.

## He was famous and popular.

But when he got home to New Zealand at the end of the year, something didn't feel right. "Why am I sad?" he wondered.

He asked a counsellor for advice.

"It's okay to feel that way," the counsellor said. "You need a plan for when things go quiet. It's a sign of strength that you told someone how you feel. This will pass. **Just be you, and you'll be fine.**"

That advice came right on time. Israel was about to face his biggest test yet.

# UFC 234
# 10 February 2019

Do you remember the fighter who inspired Israel to make it to the UFC? It was Anderson Silva. Anderson is one of the best fighters in history — unbeaten for seven years!

Israel fought him at UFC 234. **Could he beat his hero?**

Gbe body! In round one, Israel moved like the dancing fighter he is … dodged, weaved, jabbed, hooked … a spinning kick just missed.

In round two, Israel's punches began to hurt. They're like snake bites. They spring. **They sting.**

In round three, Anderson tried to knock Israel out with a flying knee. But Israel saw it coming, ducked and skipped away smiling.

## PEOWNNNNNN!

"The winner … by unanimous decision …" read the announcer, "Israel,

## 'The Last Stylebender', Adesanya!"

Israel kneeled in front of Anderson and bowed his head in respect.

Anderson bowed back. "It's your time now," he said.

He's boring
BROKENNATIVE

It's not easy being a famous person. Some people say mean things about you on social media and in public. That's happened to Israel lots of times.

"Izzy thinks he's the man, but he's trash," wrote one person.

"He's boring," said another.

"Stylebender is fake!" wrote someone else.

How does Israel cope with negative comments?

**"I don't listen to them,"** he says. "I look in the mirror and I tell myself good things. **And I surround myself with good people who keep it real with me."**

# How Naija is Israel?

Naija is another name for Nigeria. Although Israel has lived most of his life in Aotearoa–New Zealand, **he's a proud Naija too.**

He has a map of Africa tattooed on his chest. Nigeria is outlined to make it stand out.

"You look at my chest and you can see where I'm from," Israel says. "I feel like Superman when I rock it and I don't need an 'S' on my chest. I've got Africa with me."

Israel's favourite Nigerian food is suya, which is a skewer of spicy, smoky beef, eaten with tomatoes, lettuce, onions, and lime juice. "I like suya that's cooked on the streets at night time and wrapped in newspaper," he says.

One of his favourite Naija sayings is, "Naija no dey." What does it mean? **"Nigerians never come last,"** he says. **"Ever!"**

Here's some other famous Naija: Sade (singer), Hakeem Olajuwon (NBA basketball player), Chimamanda Ngozi Adichie (writer), Wale (rapper), Kamaru Usman (UFC welterweight champion).

ÆVNAT

# UFC 243
# 6 October 2019

Tonight, Israel fights for the UFC middleweight title. His opponent is Robert **'The Reaper'** Whittaker.

Israel wants to dance as part of his walk out. This time the UFC says he can. **Boom! Tick! Boom-tick! Boom! Tick! Boom-tick-tick! Flex-spin-bodies as machine guns-pukana!**

It's the biggest moment of Israel's life.

The announcer shouts into his microphone:

## "Iiiiiiiiiiiit's … tiiiiiiiiime!"

Robert has one goal: to knock Israel out. In round one, he lunges, swings, kicks … but Israel is too fast and skilful.

Round two. Gbe body! Israel knows how to move his body, move his feet, move his soul. Right jab-left hook … The Reaper is down!

## "And newwwwww … UFC middleweight champion of the world … Israel – The Last Stylebender – Adesanya!"

Israel's family scramble into the Octagon and hug him.

He lays the shiny title belt on the floor and bows to his parents.

**"I told you I'd do it!"** he says.

## "I can go anywhere and be anything in my imagination!"

**Reading challenges. Racism. Bullying. Doubts.**

Israel jabbed, kneed, punched and spin-kicked all of those opponents.

Everything he imagined has come true: joining the UFC, beating the toughest fighters in the world, **becoming the champ!**

"I always knew I could do it," he says.

But to Israel there's more to life than fighting. "The main thing for me is **learning to love myself,**" he says. "**And being happy with who I am.**"

Your imagination is powerful too.

What do you dream of doing in your life?

Israel would encourage you to back yourself, be you … and go for it!

### You'll be happy that you did.

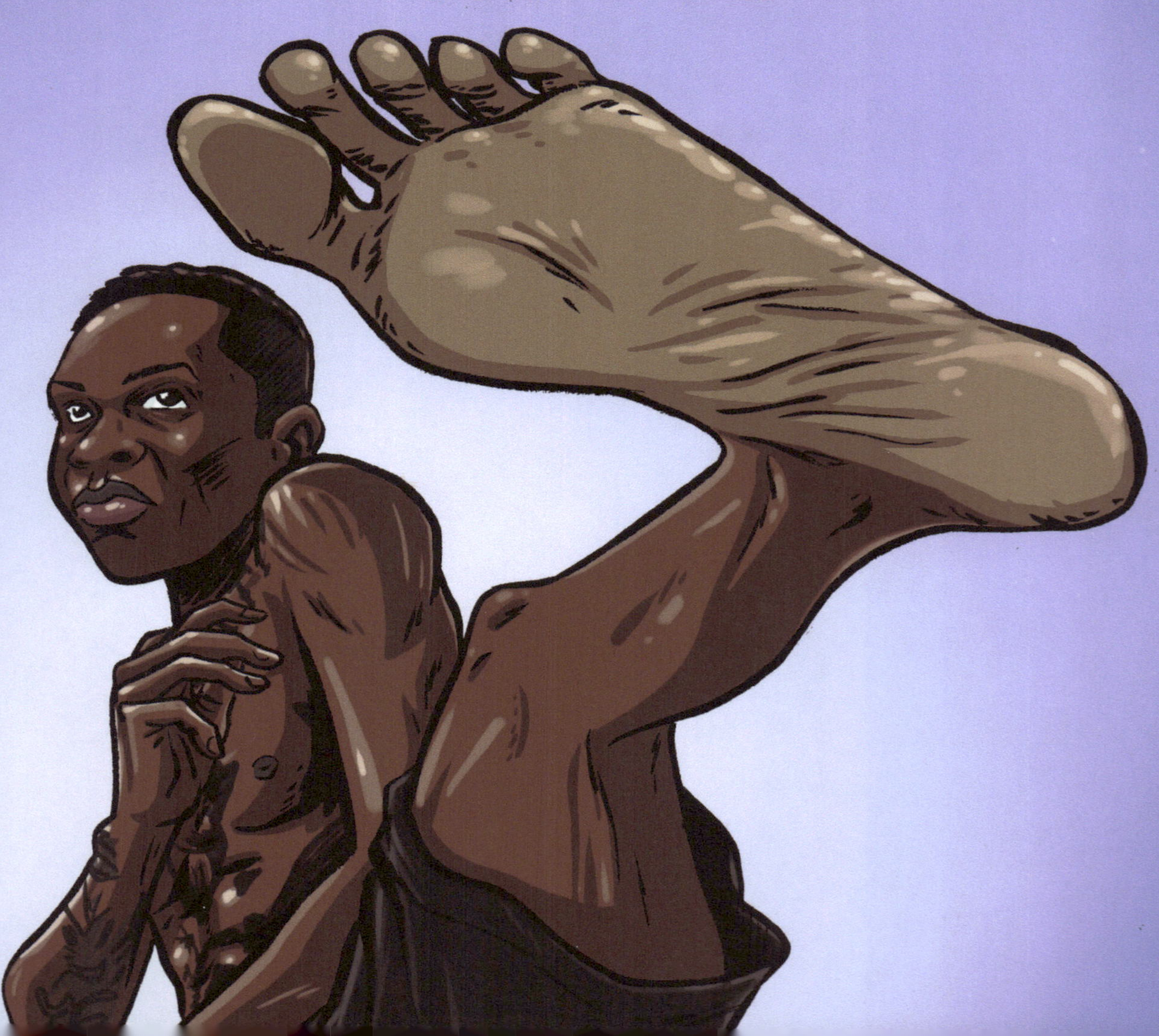